HAL•LEONARD
INSTRUMENTAL
PLAY-ALONG

AUDIO
ACCESS
INCLUDED

PLAYBACK+
Speed • Pitch • Balance • Loop

TENOR SAX

THE BEATLES

Cover Photo: Fiona Adams/Getty

To access audio visit:
www.halleonard.com/mylibrary

Enter Code
6892-2265-6816-8132

Audio Arrangements by Peter Deneff

ISBN 978-1-4950-9069-1

HAL•LEONARD®

7777 W. BLUEMOUND RD. P.O. BOX 13819 MILWAUKEE, WI 53213

In Australia Contact:
Hal Leonard Australia Pty. Ltd.
4 Lentara Court
Cheltenham, Victoria, 3192 Australia
Email: ausadmin@halleonard.com.au

Visit Hal Leonard Online at
www.halleonard.com

ALL YOU NEED IS LOVE

TENOR SAX

Words and Music by JOHN LENNON
and PAUL McCARTNEY

BLACKBIRD

TENOR SAX

Words and Music by JOHN LENNON
and PAUL McCARTNEY

DAY TRIPPER

TENOR SAX

Words and Music by JOHN LENNON
and PAUL McCARTNEY

ELEANOR RIGBY

TENOR SAX

Words and Music by JOHN LENNON
and PAUL McCARTNEY

GET BACK

TENOR SAX

Words and Music by JOHN LENNON
and PAUL McCARTNEY

HERE, THERE AND EVERYWHERE

TENOR SAX

Words and Music by JOHN LENNON
and PAUL McCARTNEY

HEY JUDE

TENOR SAX

Words and Music by JOHN LENNON
and PAUL McCARTNEY

I WILL

TENOR SAX

Words and Music by JOHN LENNON
and PAUL McCARTNEY

LET IT BE

TENOR SAX

Words and Music by JOHN LENNON
and PAUL McCARTNEY

LUCY IN THE SKY WITH DIAMONDS

TENOR SAX

Words and Music by JOHN LENNON
and PAUL McCARTNEY

OB-LA-DI, OB-LA-DA

TENOR SAX

Words and Music by JOHN LENNON
and PAUL McCARTNEY

PENNY LANE

TENOR SAX

Words and Music by JOHN LENNON
and PAUL McCARTNEY

SOMETHING

TENOR SAX

Words and Music by
GEORGE HARRISON

TICKET TO RIDE

TENOR SAX

Words and Music by JOHN LENNON
and PAUL McCARTNEY

YESTERDAY

TENOR SAX

Words and Music by JOHN LENNON
and PAUL McCARTNEY